Discover Ancient Civilizations

Creative Activities for Ancient History Classes

Written by Rebecca Stark

Illustrated by Karen Sigler and Koryn Agnello

Note: This book was originally part of the
Creative Ventures Series.

ISBN 1-56644-074-2

© 2000 Educational Impressions, Inc.

EDUCATIONAL IMPRESSIONS, INC.
Hawthorne, New Jersey 07507

Printed in the U.S.A.

Contents

To the Teacher

This resource teaches students about archaeology and provides opportunities for exploring a variety of ancient civilizations. The open-ended activities were designed to extend the imagination and creativity of your students and to encourage students to examine their feelings and values. Specifically, they focus upon the cognitive and affective pupil behaviors described in Williams' Model: fluent thinking, flexible thinking, original thinking, elaborative thinking, risk-taking, complexity, curiosity, and imagination. (See Williams' Model below).

Students must learn to recognize problems and to produce and consider a variety of alternate solutions to those problems. Teachers, therefore, should urge students to defer judgment of their ideas until they have produced many alternatives. They should also encourage them to let their imaginations run wild so that their ideas include clever, unusual alternatives as well as the more obvious ones.

Rebecca Stark

A Summary of Williams' Model

COGNITIVE-INTELLECTIVE

Fluent thinking— to generate a great number of relevant responses.

Flexible thinking— to take different approaches in order to generate different categories of thought.

Original thinking— to think in novel or unique ways in order to produce unusual responses and clever ideas.

Elaborative thinking— to add on to, or embellish upon, an idea.

AFFECTIVE-FEELING

Risk-taking— to have courage to expose yourself to failure or criticism and to defend your ideas.

Complexity— to be challenged to seek alternatives and to delve into intricate problems or ideas.

Curiosity— to be inquisitive and to be willing to follow hunches just to see what will happen.

Imagination— to feel intuitively and to reach beyond sensual or real boundaries.

Archaeology

Archaeology is the systematic retrieval and study of the material remains of past human life. The remains archaeologists study include everything made by human beings. The word used to describe these objects produced or shaped by human workmanship is "artifacts."

Archaeologists often search for artifacts by digging out a site layer by layer. This method is called stratigraphy.

Fill in the artifacts that might be found from Twentieth- and Twenty-first-Century America.

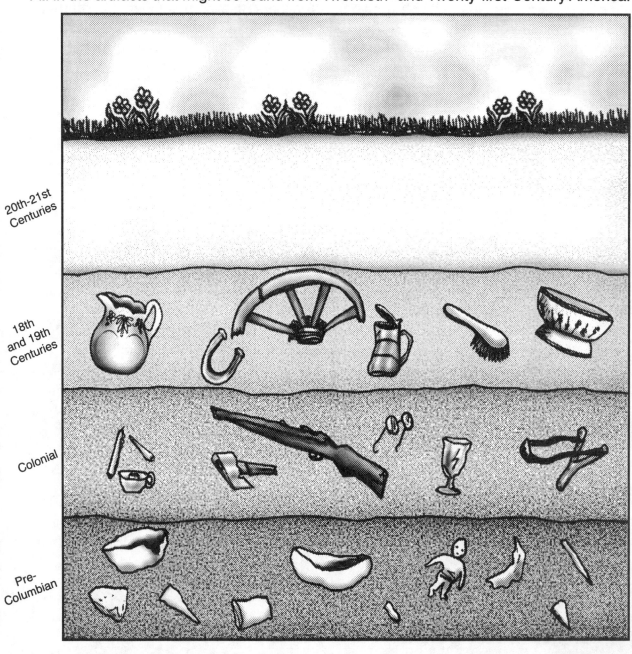

Amateur Archaeologist

Pretend that you are an amateur accompanying several archaeologists on a dig. The archaeologists have left you alone at the site. You find what appears to be a very important artifact—an entire vase! You are not sure what you should do.

Restate you problem:

_____

_____

_____

List all of your alternatives:

_____

_____

_____

_____

_____

_____

Which alternative would you choose? Why?

_____

_____

_____

_____

_____

_____

_____

Pottery of the Past

Pottery and potsherds, or bits of shattered pottery, are very useful to archaeologists. List all the things that pottery might teach us about the people who made it.

_____

_____

_____

_____

_____

_____

_____

_____

_____

_____

_____

_____

_____

                                         _____

                                         _____

                                         _____

                          _____

                          _____

                          _____

                          _____

Help Wanted!

An archaeologist has hired you to write an ad to recruit other archaeologists and amateur assistants to accompany him/her on an expedition expected to last at least one year.

List the personal characteristics and qualifications the applicants should have.

_____

_____

_____

_____

_____

_____

_____

_____

Now write 2 different ads you might place to recruit individuals with the qualities you listed above.

_____	_____
_____	_____
_____	_____
_____	_____
_____	_____
_____	_____
_____	_____

Say It with Similes

What are the qualities of a good archaeologist?

A simile is a stated comparison between two dissimilar things. The word "like" or "as" is used to make the comparison. Try to think of some unusual similes.

A good archaeologist is as...

smart as _____ .

persistent as _____ .

patient as _____ .

inquisitive as _____ .

Now add 5 more of your own.

_____ as _____ .

_____ as _____ .

_____ as _____ .

_____ as _____ .

_____ as _____ .

Note: You may change the format to include "like" instead of "as."

The Dead Sea Scrolls

The so-called Dead Sea Scrolls were found in 1947 along the shores of the Dead Sea in Jordan. A young Bedouin shepherd had been looking for his stray goat. While looking in a cave, the shepherd and his companions found rows of clay jars. In the jars were rolls of leather and papyrus, wrapped in linen. This discovery was one of the world's most important archaeological finds. Among the scrolls was the entire book of Isaiah in Hebrew from the first century B.C. It was about 1,000 years older than any previously found manuscript of the Hebrew Old Testament.

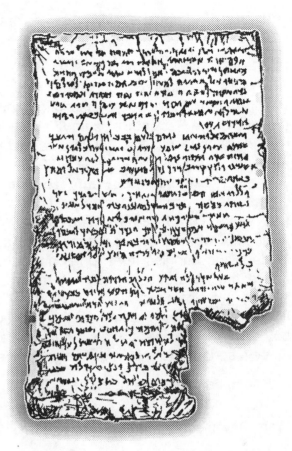

Like many other important archaeological finds, the discovery of the Dead Sea Scrolls was completely accidental.

Hypothesize, or guess, as to the possible events leading up to the following headline. Be original!

STUDENT FROM _____
MAKES IMPORTANT ARCHAEOLOGICAL FIND!

_____

_____

_____

_____

_____

_____

_____

The Behistun Rock

The writing of ancient Mesopotamia (present-day Iran and Iraq) is called cuneiform, which means "wedge-shaped." It was inscribed on tablets of soft clay by an instrument—at first probably a sharpened reed—which left wedge-shaped impressions.

The key to deciphering cuneiform writing was a triple inscription in Babylonian, Old Persian, and Elamite. The inscription and an accompanying bas-relief were carved on the face of the Rock of Behistun (Bīsitūn), a 1,700-foot cliff. The inscription recorded the way in which Darius I of Persia defeated the rebels and assumed the throne c. 522 B.C. A young Englishman, Lt. Henry Rawlinson, copied the inscriptions over a period of several years (1845–1847). The Babylonian inscription was difficult to reach. He brought ladders and dangled from ropes about 500' above the valley floor; however, he wasn't able to get close enough to it. In 1847 he hired a native boy to climb up the rock; the boy hung on by his fingers and toes and made a squeeze (a cast in wet pulped paper).

Behistun Rock: inscription and bas-relief

Rawlinson and the boy both risked their lives to decipher the inscription.

From Rawlinson's point of view, restate your problem:

_____

_____

List as many alternate solutions to the problem as you can. Be original!

_____

_____

_____

_____

_____

_____

_____

_____

The Winged Bull of Mesopotamia

In 1845 Sir Austen Henry Layard began excavation of Numrud in Iraq. He mistook the site for Ninevah. What he discovered were the remains of palaces from the ninth and seventh centuries B.C. Included were many sculptures and other important artifacts. One of the most valuable was a great winged bull.

How do you think the Arabian workers hired by Layard felt when they first saw the head rising from the ground? Compile a list of adjectives and/or phrases to describe their feelings.

_____   _____

_____   _____

_____   _____

_____   _____

_____   _____

Hypothesize, or guess, what they might have thought was happening.

_____

_____

Write a conversation between 2 of the workers.

Worker #1:_____

Worker #2:_____

Worker #1:_____

Worker #2:_____

Worker #1:_____

Worker #2:_____

Egypt: the Gift of the Nile

The great civilization of ancient Egypt was based upon a prosperous farming economy. The farming year was divided into three seasons, based upon the behavior of the Nile River. The inundation, or flood season, lasted from June through September. During this period of time the peasants worked on the great building projects. They were able to move the huge blocks of stone by floating them down the river. From October to February, when the waters receded, the peasants sowed their crops and dug their ditches. The crops were harvested during the third season—the drought season—which lasted from March through May.

The Nile River was all-important to the ancient Egyptians. Keeping this in mind, think of as many nicknames for the Nile as you can. Put a ✓ next to your best idea.

_____

_____

_____

_____

_____

_____

_____

_____

_____

_____

_____

_____

_____

_____

The Discovery of King Tut's Tomb

In 1917 archaeologist Howard Carter and his crew, hired by wealthy Englishman Lord Carnarvon, began their excavation of the Valley of the Kings in Egypt. Most archaeologists believed there was nothing left to find; however, Carter felt certain that the tomb of Tutankhamun, the "boy king" who ruled over 3,000 years ago, was still there.

Carter mapped the valley and divided it into sections. Carefully, he and his crew searched each section and marked it off on the map. Years passed, but still Carter did not give up.

Finally, on November 4, 1922, his workers found some steps. Two days later Carter found a sealed doorway at the bottom of the steps. Carter had the crew refill the stairway and posted a guard. He sent the following telegram to Lord Carnarvon: "At last you have made a wonderful discovery in valley. A magnificent tomb with seals intact. Have re-covered same for your arrival. Congratulations. Carter."

It took months to photograph, label, mend, pack, and ship the contents of the first room alone! Although he was curious to see what was beyond the sealed doorway and especially to see if King Tutankhamun himself were there, Carter knew that he had to be systematic. Two years later, his work was finally complete.

List as many adjectives as you can to describe the personality characteristics of Howard Carter.

_____   _____

_____   _____

_____   _____

_____

Now use your ideas to write an acrostic poem about Carter. An acrostic is a poem in which the first letter of each line spells a name or message.

C _____

A _____

R _____

T _____

E _____

R _____

But They're Mine!

Lord Carnarvon and Howard Carter disagreed over what should be done with the artifacts they had found. Carter thought they should all be given to the Cairo Museum. Carnarvon wanted to retain some of the less important ones for the expedition.

You are the head of an archaeological expedition that has unearthed great treasures. What will you do with them?

Restate your problem: _____

_____

List all of your alternatives:

_____

_____

_____

_____

_____

Draw a picture in the box that shows which alternative you would choose.

Vengeance of Tut's Ka

It was written in the *Book of the Dead* that the preservation of the body of the dead was necessary for the continued existence of the soul, or *ka.* It was also believed that the *ka* returned to animate the dead body after a period of 3,000 years.

At the time of the excavations, many believed that those who disturbed those ancient tombs would incur the wrath of the gods. When Lord Carnarvon died of a mosquito bite shortly after the discovery of King Tutankhamun's tomb, the superstitious were convinced that the spirit of the dead king resented his interference and caused his death!

Write two letters to the editor of a newspaper as if written the day after Lord Carnarvon's death: first from the point of view of a believer of the superstition and then from that of a nonbeliever.

Dear Editor:	Dear Editor:
_____	_____
_____	_____
_____	_____
_____	_____
_____	_____
_____	_____
_____	_____
_____	_____
_____	_____
Sincerely,	Sincerely,
_____	_____

A Delicate Balance

The ancient Egyptians, like many ancient peoples, believed in an afterlife. They believed that at death a feather, the symbol of *maat* (truth and justice), was weighed against the dead person's heart by the gods. Osiris, the god of the dead, examined the balance and gave the final verdict.

List all of your good deeds and your bad. How do you think Osiris would judge you?

<u>Good Deeds</u>	<u>Bad Deeds</u>
_____	_____
_____	_____
_____	_____
_____	_____
_____	_____
_____	_____

The Verdict: _____

_____

_____

_____

_____

From Here to Eternity

The ancient Egyptians buried with their dead all of the objects they felt would be needed in their afterlives.

What 10 objects would you want buried with you to insure a happy afterlife?

1. _____

2. _____

3. _____

4. _____

5. _____

6. _____

7. _____

8. _____

9. _____

10. _____

Worthy of Immortality

During the Pyramid Age (c. 2780 to c. 2650 B.C.) the ancient Egyptians believed that a heavenly immortality was reserved for kings and nobles. Even they, however, had to convince Osiris, the god of the dead, that they were worthy; otherwise, they would dwell with the commoners in the underground realm of Osiris.

They convinced Osiris by having their good deeds inscribed on the walls of their tombs. They also specifically listed all the sins which they had *not* committed! By about 2250 B.C. this heavenly immortality was believed to be open to anyone whom Osiris judged to be moral. Some people resorted to magic to try to gain entry into the heavens. Formulas, spells, chants, and passwords were written in the coffin lids for the dead to study and recite to Osiris upon memorization. They are known as the coffin texts. Later on these spells were written on papyrus and placed in the coffins. They have been saved in a collection now called the *Book of the Dead.*

Write a coffin text that would convince Osiris that you are deserving of immortality.

_____

_____

_____

_____

_____

_____

_____

_____

_____

_____

_____

_____

Immortality for Sale

By about 2000 B.C. Egyptian priests had begun to sell books of formulas which were guaranteed to lead to immortality. Later on they even left blank spaces for the purchaser to fill in with his or her name. The forms stated that the owner was righteous and worthy of admission into the heavens.

Pretend that you are the owner of a business that manufactures and sells the forms described above. Think of appropriate names for your business. Put a ✓ next to the name you like best.

_____

_____

_____

_____

_____

In the boxes, sketch ideas for posters advertising your product.

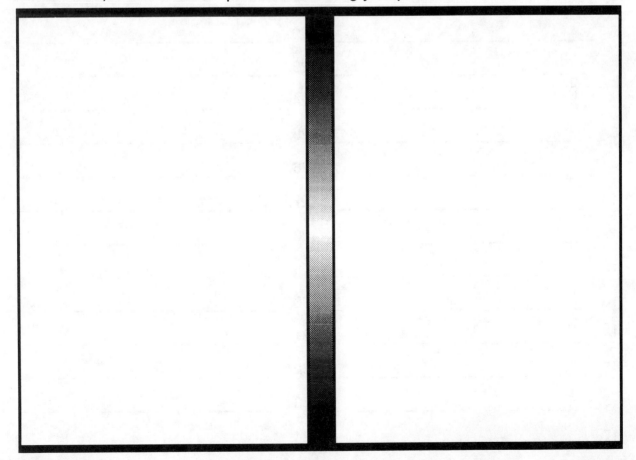

Hidden in Hieroglyphic

The system of writing of ancient Egypt in which pictorial symbols were used to represent words or sounds is called hieroglyphics. The individual picture or symbol used in this writing is called a hieroglyph or a hieroglyphic.

How many words (3 or more letters each) can you make from the letters in the word "hieroglyphic"? Try to get at least 30.

H-I-E-R-O-G-L-Y-P-H-I-C

1. _____

2. _____

3. _____

4. _____

5. _____

6. _____

7. _____

8. _____

9. _____

10. _____

11. _____

12. _____

13. _____

14. _____

15. _____

16. _____

17. _____

18. _____

19. _____

20. _____

21. _____

22. _____

23. _____

24. _____

25. _____

26. _____

27. _____

28. _____

29. _____

30. _____

31. _____

32. _____

33. _____

34. _____

Apis, the Sacred Bull of Egypt

Apis was the sacred bull worshiped at Memphis. His worship was widespread, for he was believed to be the avatar, or reincarnation, of the great god Osiris. The bull chosen for the honor of becoming Apis had to have certain markings: a black hide with a white triangular shape on its forehead, a half-moon on its right side, and a knot like a beetle under its tongue. Once chosen, the bull was regarded as a god and treated as such. There was a drawback, however. It would not be allowed to live more than 25 years. If it reached that age, it was ceremoniously drowned in the waters of the Nile. Its death was mourned until a new bull was found. Then the mourning turned to celebration!

Write a conversation between two bulls upon learning of the death of Apis: one bull has the proper markings and one does not.

Bull #1: _____

_____

Bull #2: _____

_____

Bull #1: _____

_____

Bull #2: _____

_____

Bull #1: _____

_____

Bull #2: _____

_____

Bull #1: _____

_____

Bull #2: _____

_____

Note: Apis was the name given to the sacred bull by the Greeks. The Egyptians called it Hap.

What Can You Make of Ankh?

The ankh (a cross shaped like a **T** with a loop at the top) was an important religious symbol of ancient Egypt.

See what you can make of these ankhs. Be creative!

"Worth Its Weight in Salt"

Four great trading empires grew in the open savanna plains of West Africa in the area known as the Sudan. They are Ghana (c. A.D. 700–c. A.D. 1200); Mali (c.1200–c.1500), which absorbed Ghana and extended it westward; Songhai (c.1350–c.1600), which slowly occupied the territory of Mali; and Kanem-Bornu (c.800–c.1800), which grew in the interior. These merchant traders grew prosperous by importing salt mined in the north and trading it for gold from the local mines.

Salt, necessary for life, became one of the most important commodities of African trade. The Sahara was the main source. The salt had to be extracted by pouring water into the earth in order to leach out the salt. When the water evaporated, a residue of salt was left; it was then scooped out and packed into blocks. In other places salt occurred in pure deposits, which could be quarried.

Salt became so valuable that in many cases it was literally "worth its weight in gold."

Write an acrostic poem about salt.

S _____

A _____

L _____

T _____

Animal-Tricksters of African Folklore

The civilizations of ancient Africa were rich in oral tradition. The history, mythology, and folklore were passed from one generation to the next by storytellers. Usually one of the oldest persons in the village, the storyteller enlivened the tales by adding music and sound effects.

Folktales were an important part of the oral tradition. They served not only as entertainment but also as a means of teaching social norms and morality. Animal-trickster tales were most common. Three well-known animal-tricksters of African folklore are the tortoise, the hare, and the spider. Anansi the Spider is probably the best known of all.

The animal-tricksters used their ingenuity for greedy and mischievous purposes; nevertheless, because they often outwitted larger and stronger animals, these characters usually had the sympathy of the audience. Read a few African folktales featuring the hare, the tortoise, and/or the spider.

Create an original tale featuring one of these characters.

_____

_____

_____

_____

_____

_____

_____

_____

_____

_____

_____

_____

Rewrite your story in picture-book form for young children.

EXTRA: You might want to present your story orally to your class or perhaps to a younger class. Add appropriate sound effects to enhance your presentation.

Pericles

One of the greatest of all Athenians was Pericles, who led the Athenians for 30 years. Although he was extremely powerful, he never overstepped the laws of democracy. He was only one of ten generals, but he was elected every year for 30 years!

Through a new discovery in time travel, you are able to travel back in time to the Athens of 450 B.C. to interview Pericles. What ten questions would you most like to ask him?

1. _____

_____

2. _____

_____

3. _____

_____

4. _____

_____

5. _____

_____

6. _____

_____

7. _____

_____

8. _____

_____

9. _____

_____

10. _____

_____

Education in Ancient Athens

Boys in ancient Athens began their education at about six years of age. They were taught reading, writing, and arithmetic by *grammatistes.* They were also taught music and gymnastics, which included wrestling, running, jumping, boxing, and javelin and discus throwing. At age fourteen the boys of lower-class families usually left school to work at their trade with their fathers. Those of the middle and upper classes usually continued their education. If they could afford it, they were taught by specialists who traveled from city to city, called Sophists.

Girls in ancient Athens received no education other than the care of the home and other domestic matters. Girls and women seldom left the house. When they did, a chaperon accompanied them. Although ancient Athens was considered a democracy, women and slaves (captives of war) had no say in the government.

Suppose that through a miracle of time travel, a brother and sister of the twenty-first century find themselves in ancient Athens in 432 B.C., during the great Age of Pericles. Write two entries for a diary: first from the boy's point of view and then from the girl's. Dear Diary, _____ _____ _____ _____ _____ Dear Diary, _____ _____ _____ _____ _____ _____	Now write entries for the diaries of a brother and sister of ancient Athens who find themselves in Twenty-first-Century America. Dear Diary, _____ _____ _____ _____ _____ _____ Dear Diary, _____ _____ _____ _____ _____

28   *Discovering Ancient Civilizations*   © Educational Impressions, Inc.

The Olympic Games

The love of athletics was an important unifying force among the ancient Greeks. The most important athletic events were the Olympic Games. At one time scholars believed the first games were held in Olympia in 776 B.C.; however, today many think some type of games were held even earlier.

The Olympic games were held every four years. They began at the time of the full moon of August and lasted for 7 days. The victors' only rewards were laurel wreaths, but to win was so prestigious that athletes trained for years and came from all parts of Greece to take part in the events.

Invent a new sport that could become a future Olympic event.

Is it a team or individual sport? _____

What's the objective? _____

Describe the uniforms and equipment. _____

_____

What are the most important rules? _____

_____

Is it like any other sport? _____

What are some possible names for your sport? Circle the one you like best.

_____

_____

Draw a picture to illustrate your sport.

Greek Gods and Goddesses

The ancient Greeks, like other primitive peoples, believed that their lives were subject to external powers beyond their control. These powers took the form of gods and goddesses, who were believed to be immortal.

IMPORTANT GREEK GODS & GODDESSES

Zeus—Supreme ruler of gods; heavens; earth; and air

Hera—Queen of the gods

Hades—Underworld

Poseidon—Ocean

Demeter—Agriculture

Apollo—Archer; prophecy; music

Artemis—Moon; the chase (hunt)

Hephaestus—Fire; metal-working; pottery

Athene (Athena)—Wisdom

Ares—War

Aphrodite—Love and beauty

Hermes—Messenger; commerce; skill; science

Hestia—The hearth

Choose two gods and/or goddesses of ancient Greece. You do not have to limit yourself to those listed above. List the attributes, or qualities, of the deities you have chosen. Combine some of the attributes of each to create a new deity.

Deity #1 Attributes	Deity #2 Attributes	Deity #3 Attributes
_____	_____	_____
_____	_____	_____
_____	_____	_____
_____	_____	_____
_____	_____	_____
_____	_____	_____
_____	_____	_____

Write a myth based upon your new god or goddess.

In Defense of Prometheus

The ancient Greeks believed in many gods and goddesses, but the most important of all was Zeus. Zeus was extreme in both his rewards and his punishments. One of the most famous of all punishments in Greek mythology was Zeus's punishment of Prometheus for his defiance. Among other things, Prometheus had given humankind the gift of fire—a gift Zeus believed should have been reserved for the gods. Zeus ordered that Prometheus be captured and bound in chains to a rock on Mount Caucacus. There Prometheus would remain as an eagle picked at his liver, which grew back as soon as it was devoured. As Prometheus was immortal, he would not die. Instead he would live in constant pain.

You are Prometheus's defense attorney.

What questions will you ask Zeus?

1. _____

2. _____

3. _____

4. _____

5. _____

What questions will you ask Prometheus?

1. _____

2. _____

3. _____

4. _____

5. _____

Answers the questions from the point of view of each. Prepare a summary statement to recite to the jury.

The Will of the Gods

The ancient Greeks interpreted the will of the gods in a number of ways. One custom, especially in cases of sudden emergency, was the use of augury, or interpretation of signs. For example, sometimes the augury was based on the direction in which a bird was observed to fly overhead. If the bird flew to the right of the augur as he faced north, good luck would follow; if it flew to the left of the augur, bad luck would follow.

Another custom was the consulting of oracles. Apollo, as a symbol of the light of the sun in the sense of an all-seeing and all-knowing power, was regarded as the great god of oracles. Delphi was the main center of his activity. The oracle prophesied by uttering words and sounds while in a state of frenzy. Persons educated in deciphering her prophecies put the sounds into verse. Usually, however, they stated the prophecies in such a cunning way that there was a double meaning. In that way, if a prophecy did not come true, the oracle and her priests could blame it on the way it was interpreted.

You are a famous oracle. You have been asked for advice on a current issue. You want to be sure you can say your prophecy was correct no matter what happens.

Issue: _____

Prophecy: _____

Meaning #1: _____

_____

Meaning #2: _____

_____

The Price of Pride

Arachne, who was an excellent weaver, challenged the goddess Athene (Athena) to see who was better. Athene was angered by the challenge and became even more angry when Arachne wove scenes representing the loves of the gods and goddesses into her cloth. When Athene could find no fault with the work, her anger turned to rage. She tore the cloth into shreds and threw the pieces at Arachne. By this time Arachne had become so ashamed that she hanged herself. Athene cut her down and brought her back to life; however, she punished her by turning her into a spider and her rope into a web, which Arachne forever would have to spin.

Imagine what it would feel like to be a spider. List all the adjectives that describe how you would feel if you were Arachne.

_____

_____

_____

_____

_____

_____

_____

_____

_____

_____

_____

_____

_____

_____

The 12 Labours of Heracles

Heracles belongs in the group of early heroes distinguished for their extraordinary adventures and services in the cause of human civilization. The goddess Hera hated Heracles; therefore, she arranged it so the oracle at Delphi would tell him that he must perform 10 labours, or tasks, which King Eurystheus would set up. Hera went to the king and told him to give Heracles tasks that no mortal could do and to be sure that he died doing them.

Nevertheless, Heracles completed the 10 tasks and went back to King Eurystheus to claim his freedom. The king was furious that Heracles had not died. He claimed that two of the tasks did not count and added two more. When Heracles completed those tasks as well, he won his freedom and the right to immortality.

THE TWELVE LABOURS OF HERACLES

1. Bring back the skin of the Nemean Lion;
2. Slaughter the Hydra;
3. Bring back Artemis's beautiful hind with golden antlers;
4. Catch the Erymanthian Boar;
5. Cleanse the stable of King Augeas;
6. Get rid of the Stymphalian Birds;
7. Capture the Cretan Bull;
8. Fetch the man-eating mares of Diomedes;
9. Get the girdle (belt) of Hippolyta, queen of the Amazons;
10. Steal the cattle of the 3-headed ogre, Geryon;
11. Bring back the golden apples of the Hesperides; and
12. Bring back Cerberus, the Hound of Hades.

Invent 12 more labours for Heracles.

The Riddle of the Sphinx

The Sphinx of Greek mythology was a monster with the face of a woman; the breast, feet, and tail of a lion; and the wings of a bird. She had been sent by the goddess Hera to afflict the city of Thebes. The Sphinx crouched on the top of a rock and detained all travelers who came her way. She would not let them pass safely unless they could correctly answer a riddle she proposed. For a long time, no one succeeded. Every traveler she encountered was killed. At last Oedipus approached. The Sphinx asked him, "Who is it that walks on four feet, then on two feet, and then on three feet?" Oedipus replied, "Man, who in childhood creeps on hands and knees, in manhood walks erect, and in old age with the aid of a staff." The Sphinx was so mortified at the solving of her riddle that she cast herself down from the rock and perished.

Make up as least five more riddles for the Sphinx to ask travelers.

1. _____

_____

_____

2. _____

_____

_____

3. _____

_____

_____

4. _____

_____

_____

5. _____

_____

_____

Note: Do not confuse this creature with the Sphinx of Egypt.

Messengers to the Gods

Hermes was the messenger and herald of the gods. His three most important attributes were (1) his *petasus,* or winged hat, (2) his *talaria,* the wings attached to his ankles with which he traveled at the speed of light, and (3) his *caduceus,* the wand with serpents wound around it. (He later gave his caduceus to Aesculapius, the god of medicine.)

Iris was the goddess of the rainbow. She, too, was a messenger of the gods, especially of the goddess Hera.

Hermes and Iris have joined forces to form a messenger service. Think of some possible names for their company. Be original!

1. _____

2. _____

3. _____

4. _____

5. _____

6. _____

7. _____

8. _____

9. _____

10. _____

Pus a ✓ next to the name you like best.

Create an ad for their company in the space on the right.

Gracious Gifts

When the Greek hero Perseus set out to kill the monster Medusa, he was loaned three things by the Graiae, or Gray Women, to help him get the head of the monstrous Medusa. They were the winged sandals of Hermes to give him magic speed; a magic bag, or wallet, that shrank or expanded to fit the contents; and the magic helmet of Hades, which made the wearer invisible.

For each of the following think of as many ideas as you can. Be creative and try to think of some unusual answers!

If you could borrow the winged sandals for one day, how would you use them?

_____

_____

_____

_____

_____

If you could borrow the magic wallet, or bag, for one day, how would you use it?

_____

_____

_____

_____

If you could borrow the magic helmet for one day, how would you use it?

_____

_____

_____

_____

Autobiography of a Narcissist

In the mythology of the ancient Greeks, Narcissus was the beautiful youth who fell in love with his own image when he stooped down to take a drink in a clear pond. As he had never before seen himself, he thought that the image was a beautiful water spirit. He bent down and tried to kiss the image, but each time he drew near, the image disappeared. Narcissus remained at the waterside to gaze upon the image until at last he pined away and died. The gods changed him into a beautiful flower. Today we use the term "narcissist" to describe a person who shows excessive love or admiration for him/herself.

Prepare a list of at least 10 adjectives which describe you. Put a ✓ next to the 5 that represent your best qualities.

1. _____
2. _____
3. _____
4. _____
5. _____

6. _____
7. _____
8. _____
9. _____
10. _____

Now write a brief autobiography as if you were a narcissist.

_____
_____
_____
_____
_____
_____
_____
_____

The Judgment of Paris

The myth regarding the judgment of Paris provides a mythical cause of a historical event—the Trojan War.

The day before his birth, Paris's mother, Queen Hecuba, had a terrible dream. The prophets said it meant her child would cause Troy to be set on fire and destroyed. The king, therefore, ordered that the baby Paris be taken upon its birth to Mt. Ida and left to die. But a shepherd found the baby Paris and cared for him. Paris grew up to be strong and handsome.

One day three goddesses came to Paris: Hera, Athene, and Aphrodite. At the request of Zeus, they asked him to judge which of them was the fairest. They explained that they had been at the wedding feast of Peleus and Thetis when the goddess Eris, angry that she hadn't been invited, threw a beautiful golden apple in their midst. On the apple was written "To the fairest."

Each of the three offered to give Paris a special gift if he would choose in her favor. Hera offered great power and riches; Athene offered wisdom, which he could use to win immortal fame as a hero; and Aphrodite offered him the loveliest woman on Earth. He chose Aphrodite and immediately made enemies of the other two.

The most beautiful woman on Earth was Helen, wife of Menelaus, king of Sparta. Following the advice of Aphrodite, Paris sailed to Sparta and was warmly greeted by Menelaus. When Menelaus was called away, Paris seized the opportunity to carry Helen away. Under Aphrodite's spell, Helen could not resist.

Hera sent her messenger Iris to tell Menelaus what had happened. He and his brother Agamemnon sent heralds to the other Greek heroes to summon their aid. After two years of preparation, a great fleet of over 1,000 ships was assembled and filled with soldiers. Agamemnon was in command. The Trojan War had begun!

As Paris, write your thoughts regarding the choice you must make in the form of a soliloquy. A soliloquy is a literary or dramatic discourse in which a character talks to him/herself or reveals his/her thoughts in the form of a monologue without a listener.

_____

_____

_____

_____

_____

_____

Prophecies

Years after Paris had been abandoned on Mt. Ida, he returned to Troy. When his family learned who he was, they welcomed him—except for his sister Cassandra! She had been given the gift of prophecy; unfortunately, she had offended Apollo, who had given her the gift. Apollo arranged it so that her prophecies, although true, would never be believed. She warned the Trojans in vain that if Paris were allowed to live, Troy would fall.

Suppose these prophecies were made. To what might they refer? List several ideas for each.

It will be worth ten times as much next year.

_____

_____

_____

They will not exist by the turn of the century!

_____

_____

_____

It will float into the ocean.

_____

_____

_____

She will become a great world leader.

_____

_____

_____

Describe how you would feel if you knew that you could predict the future, but no one would believe you.

_____

_____

_____

The Face That Launched
A Thousand Ships

In about 1200 B.C. the confederated (united) Greeks waged a ten-year war against Troy. Its legendary cause was the abduction of Helen, queen of Sparta, by the Trojan prince Paris. The result of the war was the burning and destruction of Troy.

Helen has been called the "face that launched a thousand ships." Create a conversation between Helen and her psychiatrist, who is trying to rid her of her feelings of guilt.

Helen: _____

_____

Psychiatrist: _____

_____

Helen: _____

_____

Psychiatrist: _____

_____

Helen: _____

_____

Psychiatrist: _____

_____

Helen: _____

_____

Psychiatrist: _____

_____

Helen: _____

_____

Witness to Disaster

In A.D. 79 Pompeii was a bustling port town. In early August tremors were felt, but they were not strong enough to cause much concern. Then, suddenly, on the morning of August 24 the earth began to shake violently. The tremors were followed by a terrifying explosion. Mt. Vesuvius had erupted!

Some people fled immediately and escaped from the area. Those who managed to survive the poisonous sulfur fumes that had formed returned to the city. They found that Pompeii was almost completely buried under volcanic ash and stones, soon to be forgotten.

Imagine that through a miracle of time travel you have met someone who witnessed the eruption of Mt. Vesuvius. What three questions will you ask him/her?

1. _____

2. _____

3. _____

In primitive cultures gods and goddesses were identified with the elements of nature over which they presided; therefore, incidents involving the elements of nature (storms, earthquakes, calm weather, etc.) were believed to result from the activities and relationships of the gods. From the point of view of the ancients, list as many reasons for the eruption of Mt. Vesuvius as possible.

_____

_____

_____

_____

_____

_____

_____

An Exciting Event!

Life in ancient Crete was good. The upper classes, at least, had a great deal of time for amusement and recreation. There were theaters for religious plays and athletic events, such as boxing and gymnastic matches. There was even a bullfighting/rodeo type of event. The sport seems to have involved an acrobat who seized a charging bull by its horns and vaulted over its head; he then did a handspring from the bull's back while a female assistant steadied the animal by holding its horns. (Some believe the activities to have occurred in opposite order.)

Think of some appropriate names for this sport/event. List as many as you can. Circle the name you like best.

_____   _____

_____   _____

_____   _____

_____   _____

_____   _____

In the boxes sketch some ideas for billboard posters to advertise an upcoming event of this type.

Alexander the Great

Many scholars view Alexander the Great as the most important figure in the ancient world. His invasion of Asia in 334 B.C. marked the beginning of world empires. At about twenty years of age, Alexander ruled virtually the entire civilized world. He united two distinct cultures—Greek and Oriental—thereby laying the foundation for a new civilization known as "Hellenistic."

When Alexander died in 323 B.C. at thirty-three years of age, the political empire he had created also collapsed; however, during his 13 years as Macedonian king he had changed the world in which he lived!

Imagine that it is 100 years from now and the entire world is ruled by one man or woman. Compile a list of adjectives to describe the ruler.

_____   _____

_____   _____

_____   _____

_____   _____

How did the ruler gain power? _____

_____

How does he/she keep that power?_____

_____

Is he/she just? _____

From the point of view of a citizen of this empire, describe how life is different from the way it was in the early twenty-first century.

_____

_____

_____

_____

The Art of Persuasion

Of all the subjects taught to the boys of ancient Greece and Rome who continued their education, one of the most important was rhetoric. Rhetoric is the art of persuasive speaking.

Think of some current issue about which you have a strong opinion. It may be a political, social, economic, or even a personal issue.

What is the issue?

_____

_____

_____

Write at least 5 facts to support your opinion.

1. _____

2. _____

3. _____

4. _____

5. _____

Now prepare a speech regarding this issue, but TAKE THE OPPOSITE POINT OF VIEW!

_____

_____

_____

_____

_____

_____

_____

The Roman Republic

From 509 B.C., when the last Etruscan king was driven out, until 31 B.C., when Octavian declared himself Emperor of Rome, Rome was a republic. The republic was ruled by two consuls who shared the power.

Imagine what it would be like if your country were ruled by two men and/or women who equally shared the power.

List all the ways in which life in your country would be different.

_____

_____

_____

_____

_____

_____

_____

Who's going first?   Who's going first?

_____

_____

_____

_____

_____

_____

_____

_____

_____

_____

"I Forbid!"

Besides the two consuls, the Romans were governed by a council known as the senate. The senators came from the most prominent families and were appointed for life. It was their responsibility to debate and determine state policy.

The senate was not all-powerful, however. Laws had to be approved by the assembly, which was made up of the populus, or ordinary people. Beginning in 496 B.C. there were also tribunes—at first two and then ten. They were plebians (commoners) who had the power to stop any action of the senate that they felt would harm the common people. All they had to do was to shout, *"Veto!"* which meant "I forbid!"

Suppose you had the power to veto any law before it was passed. What laws (in your nation, state, city, school or home) would you veto? Tell why.

Veto!

1. _____

_____

2. _____

_____

3. _____

_____

4. _____

_____

5. _____

_____

6. _____

_____

Colossal Inheritance

You have just inherited the Colosseum of Rome. What will you do with it? List your ideas.

1. _____
2. _____
3. _____
4. _____
5. _____
6. _____
7. _____
8. _____
9. _____
10. _____

11. _____
12. _____

Draw a picture of your best idea!

"Et Tu, Brute?"

One of the most famous rulers of ancient Rome was Julius Caesar. He had been a great general and politician. By 45 B.C., he had become the sole ruler of Rome. Although he governed wisely and the ordinary people liked him, many senators feared he would declare himself king. His enemies stabbed him to death in the senate on the fifteenth of March, 44 B.C. A power struggle then developed between Caesar's nephew Octavian and Mark Antony. Antony was defeated in battle in 31 B.C.

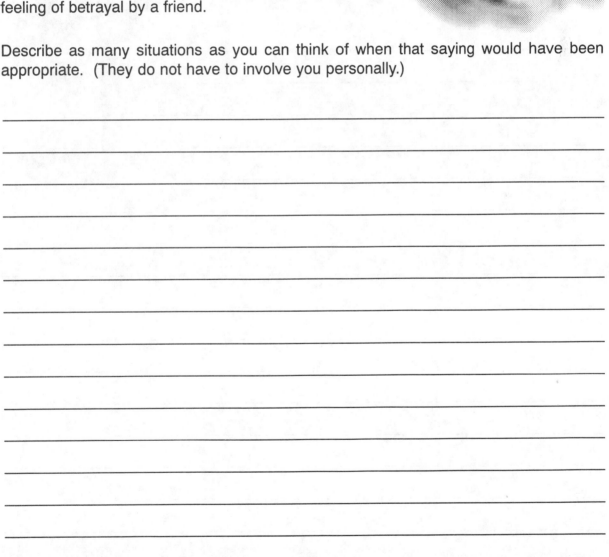

In Shakespeare's version of *Julius Caesar,* Caesar called out, *"Et tu, Brute?"* Translated from the Latin it means, "And you, Brutus?" This statement is often used to indicate a feeling of betrayal by a friend.

Describe as many situations as you can think of when that saying would have been appropriate. (They do not have to involve you personally.)

_____

_____

_____

_____

_____

_____

_____

_____

_____

_____

_____

_____

Emperor _____

From 31 B.C. until his death in A.D. 14, Octavian Caesar ruled alone, He became the first Roman Emperor. The senate gave him the title of "Augustus," which is similar in meaning to "Imperial Majesty." Augustus made many improvements throughout the empire. He appointed honest governors and trained civil-service workers to replace the corrupt officials of the past. He was also responsible for great building projects, such as roads, theaters, libraries, granaries, and baths.

Pretend that you have just been declared the first Emperor or Empress of _____. What improvements will you make?
(your city or state)

_____

_____

_____

_____

_____

_____

_____

_____

_____

_____

_____

_____

_____

_____

_____

A Fight to the Death

Gladiators were persons trained to entertain the public by engaging in mortal combat against each other or against wild beasts.

Pretend that you live in Rome during the time of Augustus's rule. Write him a letter describing your feelings about these gladitorial shows.

Dear Augustus,

_____

_____

_____

_____

_____

_____

_____

_____

_____

_____

Sincerely,

Do I Really Want to Know?

Varuna was the all-seeing god of ancient India. He was god of the seas as well as the personification of the night sky. With his 1,000 eyes, he saw and knew all. No one could keep a secret from him.

Suppose you wake up tomorrow and find that you have acquired the powers of Varuna!

What are the advantages of knowing everyone's secrets?	What are the disadvantages of knowing everyone's secrets?
_____	_____
_____	_____
_____	_____
_____	_____
_____	_____
_____	_____
_____	_____
_____	_____
_____	_____
_____	_____
_____	_____
_____	_____
_____	_____

Valkyries Wanted

Odin was the greatest of the Norse gods. Not only was he the god of war, but also of wisdom, poetry and magic. It was his responsibility to put off Ragnarök, the day of doom, when heaven and earth would be destroyed. His castle was called Valhalla. There the brave dead heroes and heroines gathered, destined to remain until Ragnarök, when they would join Odin in his losing battle against a monstrous wolf.

Odin wanted to gather as many heroes as possible so that he could face the impending disaster in glory. The Valkyries, armed and mounted war-like maidens, helped him by deciding which of the slain were deserving of Valhalla.

Sketch two recruitment posters for Odin to help him recruit Valkyries.

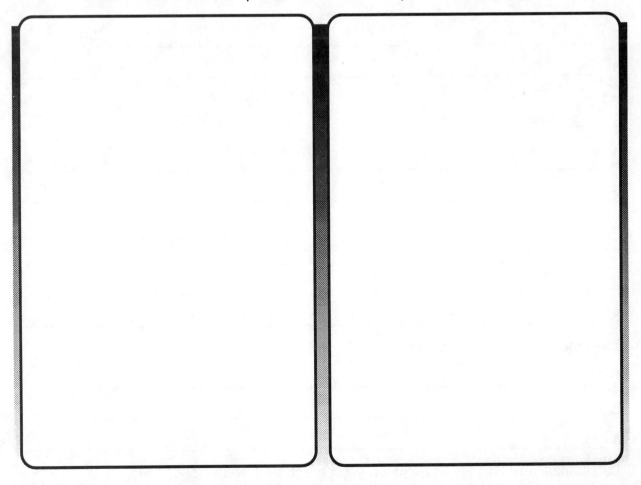

Balder the Good

Balder (Baldur), son of the great god Odin and the goddess Frigga, was the sun-god of Norse mythology. Wherever he went, he radiated peace and well-being. It so happened, however, that Balder dreamed of his impending death. Frigga, therefore, decided to make every creature that walked, crawled, swam, or flew take an oath not to harm her son. She accidentally overlooked the mistletoe, but she thought it too puny to do any harm.

Except for Odin, the gods and goddesses all believed Balder to be safe from harm. In order to honor him, they hurled weapons at him to prove his invulnerability. Each gracefully bounced off his shining body!

The evil Loki cunningly took advantage of the situation. He whittled the stem of a sprig of mistletoe until it became very sharp. Then he tricked Balder's blind brother Hoder into throwing it at Balder and killing him.

You are the district attorney investigating Balder's death. What questions will you ask…

Frigga?

1. _____

2. _____

3. _____

Hoder?

1. _____

2. _____

3. _____

Loki?

1. _____

2. _____

3. _____

The other gods and goddesses?

1. _____

2. _____

3. _____

Summarize your findings. Whom will you charge and with what crime(s)?

The Maya

The Maya civilization of southern Mexico and Central America was the most brilliant pre-Columbian civilization ever discovered. It flourished from the third century to the sixteenth century, when the Spaniards arrived.

The Maya were a brilliant people. They had invented a hieroglyphic form of writing and two different kinds of numbers (similar to the way we have Roman and Arabic numerals). They also invented a sign for zero, which Europeans didn't have until it was brought from India in the eighth century. The Maya even worked out a nearly perfect calendar.

Every 20 years (more often in large cities) the Maya set up new pyramids, palaces, and other monuments and abandoned their old ones. This went on for about 500–600 years. Then suddenly the building stopped. The village of Copán erected its final monument in A.D. 800. Tikal, the largest Mayan city, built its last one in A.D. 869. No one really knows why!

Hypothesize as to the reasons for this building and abandonment.

_____

_____

_____

_____

_____

_____

_____

_____

_____

_____

Stonehenge

Stonehenge, located on the Salisbury Plain in England, is one of the best known monuments of the ancient world. It is a large circular setting of large standing stones and comprises an area 320' in diameter. Around the stones is a low bank and around it a broken shallow ditch or moat. Inside the bank are two shallow circular ditches called the North and South Barrows; however, they are not actually barrows, or prehistoric grave mounds. Also as part of the plan are a number of holes which had been dug up and later filled up with soil and debris.

Stonehenge was probably built as a place of worship; however, the nature of the religion that was practiced there is still not known. Some who studied the monument believed it was connected with the Druids. The Druids were Celtic priests who ruled much of Europe. They came to Britain from Gaul in the fourth century B.C. It has been shown, however, that the Druids had no connection with Stonehenge. Some believe that Stonehenge was a temple for sky worship. Perhaps they are right, but as of now there is not enough clear evidence to be sure.

In the 1950s Professors Atkinson, Piggott, and Stone investigated Stonehenge. Their work resulted in the radiocarbon dating of the Aubrey Holes (named after John Aubrey, who discovered them in the 17th century) and the discovery of most of the details from which the history of Stonehenge has been pieced together. The three men, however, dug only in one half of the area covered by the monument. They left the other half alone for future archaeologists.

From the point of view of the three archaeologists, state the problem you have in deciding where and how much to dig. Describe your alternatives:

Problem: _____

Alternative #1: _____

Alternative #2: _____

Alternative #3: _____

Evaluate their choice: _____

_____

Voyage to the Past

You own a travel agency. Plan a detailed itinerary for a family interested in ancient civilizations. Be sure to include monuments to visit, modes of transportation, time allotted for each location, and other important factors.

ITINERARY

_____

_____

_____

_____

_____

_____

_____

_____

_____

_____

_____

_____

_____

_____

_____

_____

_____

_____

_____

_____

_____

_____

_____

An Acrostic

An acrostic poem is one in which the first letters of each line spell a name or message. Write an acrostic poem about the ancient civilization of your choice.

Back in Time

You have found a magic ring that enables you to travel back in time to an ancient civilization.

You can take someone with you. Whom will you take?

_____

Where will you go?

_____

What questions will you ask the leaders? (Tell which leaders.)

1. _____

2. _____

3. _____

4. _____

5. _____

What questions will you ask the ordinary citizens?

1. _____

2. _____

3. _____

4. _____

5. _____

You have only a few minutes left before you must return to your own time. What five things will you tell them about your own civilization?

1. _____

2. _____

3. _____

4. _____

5. _____

Another Sit-Com

Create a TV situation comedy that takes place in ancient times.

Where will it take place?

_____

Describe the general plot.

_____

_____

_____

_____

_____

List the main characters. Think of some actors or actresses you would cast to portray them.

_____

_____

_____

_____

Think of as many possible names for the series as you can.

_____

_____

_____

_____

What name do you like best? _____

Summarize an episode.

_____

_____

_____

_____

Headlines

You pick up the morning paper and find out that all of the articles have been cut out. Only the headlines remain. Hypothesize, or guess, the possible stories behind these headlines. Be creative and try to think of some unusual ideas!

GREAT PYRAMID OF KHUFU (CHEOPS) CHOSEN AS SITE!

_____

_____

_____

_____

OUR IDEAS OF ANCIENT WORLD ARE SHATTERED!

_____

_____

_____

_____

IMPORTANT ARCHAEOLOGICAL FIND IN (YOUR HOMETOWN)!

_____

_____

_____

_____

STUDENTS UNCOVER ARCHAEOLOGICAL HOAX!

_____

_____

_____

_____

Wonders of the Ancient World

There are seven wonders of the ancient world. They were first designated by Antipater of Sidon about 2,000 years ago.

❖❖ THE SEVEN WONDERS OF THE ANCIENT WORLD ❖❖

The Pyramids at Gizeh: The Pyramids at Gizeh (Giza) were built by three Fourth-Dynasty Pharaohs: Khufu, Khafre, and Menkaure. The Great Pyramid of Khufu was completed c. 2580 B.C.

The Temple of Artemis: The Temple of Artemis of the Ephesians was built c. 550 B.C. and rebuilt in c. 356 B.C. at Ephesus, Turkey.

The Tomb of King Mausolus: The Mausoleum, or tomb of King Mausolus, was built in Halicarnassus (modern Bodrun, Turkey) c. 325 B.C.

The Hanging Gardens: The Hanging Gardens of Babylon were constructed c. 600 B.C. within the palace at Babylon, the capital of Babylonia. They are believed to be the work of King Nebuchadrezzar II.

The Statue of Zeus: The 40-foot marble, gold, and ivory statue of Zeus was built by the sculptor Phidias c. 460 B.C. at Olympia, Greece.

The Pharos of Alexandria: This 400-foot tall lighthouse was built from c. 292 to 280 B.C., off the coast of Alexandria by Sostratus of Cnidus for Ptolemy II of Egypt.

The Colossus of Rhodes: The 105-foot bronze statue of Helios, the sun god, was sculpted by Chares from c. 292 to 280 B.C.

Only the Pyramids remain intact. Of the others, fragments remain of the Temple of Artemis and the Tomb of King Mausolus. No trace remains of the other four.

You are an archaeologist and have just discovered what future scholars will call the "Eighth Wonder of the Ancient World." Describe it. Tell where it is and how you found it. Who built it and for what reason? List several possibilities.

_____ Draw a picture of the "Eighth Wonder" here.

_____

_____

_____

_____

_____

_____

Follow-up Activities

1. Research an ancient civilization. Make a 20-card fact file about it.

2. Design a poster that shows the important tools of an archaeologist.

3. Choose one or more of the following people: Heinrich Schliemann, Sir Arthur Evans, Flinders Petrie, Paul-Émile Botta, Hiram Bingham and/or John Lloyd Stephens. Research and report on the contributions he/they made to the field or archaeology.

4. Research and report on the methods used by archaeologists to date the artifacts they find.

5. Make a flipbook of the "Seven Wonders of the Ancient World."

6. Draw a picture of the Egyptian monument called the Sphinx.

7. Research and report on the importance of the Rosetta Stone.

8. The ancient Chinese carefully guarded their secret of silk-making, for silk was their most important trading product. Research and report on the uses of silk by the ancient Chinese. Make a "how-to" booklet describing how silk was made.

9. Describe what is meant by the Code of Hammurabi and explain its importance.

10. Draw a map that represents the Inca Empire at its greatest height.

11. Compare and contrast two ancient civilizations of your choice.

12. Create a crossword puzzle based upon facts about ancient civilizations.

13. Create a word-search puzzle about ancient civilizations.

14. Find out what is meant by the codices (codex, sing.) of the ancient Maya. Write an editorial describing your opinion of their destruction by the Spanish priests.

More Follow-up Activities

15. Research the life of the ancient Greek Socrates. Find out why he was put to death.

16. Write a character sketch of Cleopatra.

17. Research the necessary requirements to become an archaeologist. Prepare an appropriate course of study for a college student who wishes to major in archaeology.